Weapons and Technology of
World War II

Windsor Chorlton

Heinemann
LIBRARY

H www.heinemann.co.uk/library
Visit our website to find out more information about Heinemann Library books.

To order:
☎ Phone 44 (0) 1865 888066
▤ Send a fax to 44 (0) 1865 314091
▢ Visit the Heinemann Bookshop at www.heinemann.co.uk/library to browse our catalogue and order online.

First published in Great Britain by Heinemann Library,
Halley Court, Jordan Hill, Oxford OX2 8EJ,
a division of Reed Educational and Professional Publishing Ltd.
Heinemann is a registered trademark of Reed Educational and Professional Publishing Ltd.

OXFORD MELBOURNE AUCKLAND
JOHANNESBURG BLANTYRE GABORONE
IBADAN PORTSMOUTH (NH) USA CHICAGO

Produced for Heinemann Library by Discovery Books Limited
Designed by Sabine Beaupré
Illustrations by Mark Franklin
Maps by Stefan Chabluk
Consultant: Stewart Ross
Originated by Dot Gradations
Printed by Wing King Tong in Hong Kong

ISBN 0 431 11996 1
05 04 03 02
10 9 8 7 6 5 4 3 2 1

British Library Cataloguing in Publication Data
Chorlton, Windsor 1948–
  Weapons and technology of World War II. – (20th century perspectives)
  1. World War, 1939–1945 – Equipment and supplies – Juvenile literature
  I. Title
  623.4'09044

Acknowledgements
The publishers would like to thank the following for permission to reproduce photographs:
Corbis, pp. 4, 6, 7, 13, 14, 15, 16, 17, 18, 19, 20, 22, 24, 25, 30, 31, 32, 35 (top and bottom), 36, 37, 38, 39, 40, 41, 42, 43; Hulton Getty, pp. 9; 27, 28, 29 (bottom), 33, 34; Peter Newark's Pictures, pp. 8, 10, 11, 26, 29 (top).

Cover photograph reproduced with permission of Corbis.

Every effort has been made to contact copyright holders of any material reproduced in this book. Any omissions will be rectified in subsequent printings if notice is given to the publishers.

Any words appearing in the text in bold, **like this**, are explained in the glossary.

Contents

Hitler on the warpath   4

Weapons of the infantry   6

Artillery   8

Tanks   10

Fighter planes   12

Bombers   14

Airborne troops   16

Warships   18

Aircraft carriers   20

Amphibious warfare   22

Submarines   24

Radar   26

Communications   28

The code-breakers   30

The propaganda weapon   32

The home front   34

Rockets and guided missiles   36

The atomic bomb   38

Medicine   40

A scientific revolution   42

Timeline   44

Further reading and places of interest   45

Glossary   46

Index   48

Hitler on the warpath

Adolf Hitler (seen here at a Nazi party rally) and the Nazis were fascists, which means they believed in complete control of society by government. They also thought their race was superior to others.

Military build-up

In World War One, which raged from 1914 to 1918 on battlefronts in Europe and beyond, Germany and its allies had been defeated. After its defeat, Germany signed the Treaty of Versailles with some of the victorious nations – Italy, France and Britain. Under this agreement, Germany was allowed only a small army, a tiny navy and no air force at all.

But when Adolf Hitler, the leader of the Nazi party, came to power in 1933, he immediately set about rearming Germany. His long-term aim was to carve out a German **empire** in the Soviet Union. The other European nations began to rearm, too, but took no direct action to stop Hitler. In 1939, the Soviet leader Josef Stalin signed a non-aggression pact with Hitler, hoping it would buy him time to build up his own armed forces.

Lightning war

Under Hitler, Germany would wage a new type of warfare. *Blitzkrieg*, meaning 'lightning war', used massed tank formations supported by aeroplanes to rip through enemy defences. The *blitzkrieg* tactic was first used with devastating effect when Germany invaded Poland in September 1939.

A war without limits

Two days after the invasion, Britain and France – known as the Allied Powers, or Allies – declared war on Germany. The next year, Hitler's army invaded and occupied France. Then, in 1941, Germany invaded the Soviet Union, having made an alliance with Japan in the hope that the Japanese would invade the Soviets from the East. Instead, Japan launched a war of expansion in the Pacific (see map on page 21). This started in December 1941 with an attack on the US fleet in Hawaii.

The USA and Canada immediately declared war on Japan. Germany and its main European ally, Italy – which together with Japan were termed the Axis Powers – in turn declared war on the USA. Two years after German tanks rolled across the Polish border, the conflict had become global. World War Two would involve 200 countries before it ended in 1945.

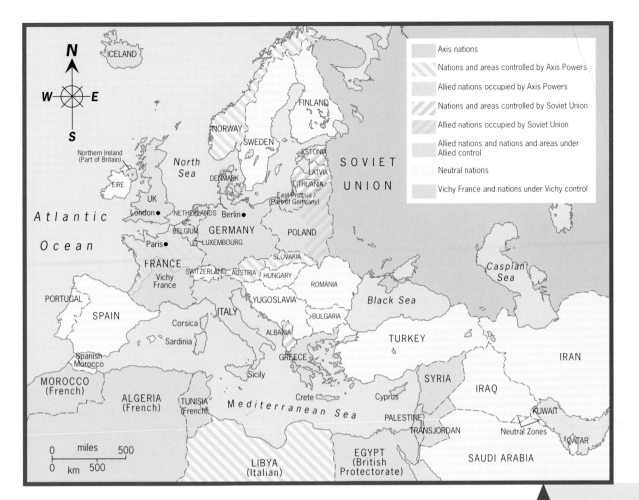

Map legend:
- Axis nations
- Nations and areas controlled by Axis Powers
- Allied nations occupied by Axis Powers
- Nations and areas controlled by Soviet Union
- Allied nations occupied by Soviet Union
- Allied nations and nations and areas under Allied control
- Neutral nations
- Vichy France and nations under Vichy control

Map labels: ICELAND, FINLAND, NORWAY, SWEDEN, ESTONIA, Northern Ireland (Part of Britain), North Sea, DENMARK, LATVIA, LITHUANIA, SOVIET UNION, EIRE, UK, London, NETHERLANDS, Berlin, East Prussia (Part of Germany), Atlantic Ocean, BELGIUM, GERMANY, POLAND, Paris, LUXEMBOURG, FRANCE, SWITZERLAND, AUSTRIA, HUNGARY, SLOVAKIA, Caspian Sea, Vichy France, ROMANIA, PORTUGAL, YUGOSLAVIA, Black Sea, SPAIN, ITALY, BULGARIA, Corsica, ALBANIA, TURKEY, Sardinia, GREECE, IRAN, Spanish Morocco, Sicily, SYRIA, IRAQ, MOROCCO (French), Crete, Cyprus, KUWAIT, ALGERIA (French), TUNISIA (French), Mediterranean Sea, PALESTINE, TRANSJORDAN, Neutral Zones, QATAR, LIBYA (Italian), EGYPT (British Protectorate), SAUDI ARABIA

0 miles 500
0 km 500

Powerful weapons

The tanks, aeroplanes and ships of World War Two were not new weapons, but they were faster and more powerfully armed than anything seen before. Radio, **radar** and other **electronic** devices made them deadlier still. Fast-moving tanks communicating by radio could win or lose battles involving millions of men in a matter of days. Long-range bombers guided by radar could navigate at night to targets deep inside enemy territory. Submarines and aircraft carriers made every part of the world a potential battlefield.

World War Two was the first conflict in which scientists made a major contribution. The war was responsible for the development of the jet engine, electronic computers, **antibiotics** and **insecticides**. The period of conflict and the time before it also produced two terrible new weapons, the atomic bomb and the **ballistic missile**.

World War Two was fought on the **home front** as well as on the battlefield. Economic power was as important as military **strategy**, and every available worker was mobilized to produce the weapons and materials that kept the conflict going. As a result, **civilians** as well as soldiers were sometimes seen as military targets.

By 1940, the Axis Powers had control of much of Europe. The Germans had occupied the northern part of France and made the southern region into a separate territory called Vichy France. The areas under control of the Vichy government sided with the Axis Powers.

Weapons of the infantry

The brunt of the fighting in World War Two was borne by the **infantry** using mainly **rifles**, machine guns and pistols to kill the enemy or to repel attackers. Most infantrymen carried a rifle, a medium-range gun accurate up to 500 metres. When infantry attacked or retreated, they were protected by covering fire from machine guns that could loose off up to 1000 **rounds** a minute.

Carbines and assault rifles

World War Two produced new types of small weapons that were compromises between the accuracy of a rifle, the portability of a pistol and the firepower of a machine gun. The Americans, for example, sacrificed accuracy for ease of handling with the M1 carbine, a rifle with a short **barrel** weighing little more than 2 kilograms. The Germans produced the MP44, an assault rifle that could fire either a single shot almost as accurately as a rifle, or bursts of fire like a machine gun.

Sub-machine guns

The sub-machine gun, first used at the end of World War One and very popular with American gangsters in the 1920s, was a cross between a pistol and a machine gun. Light enough to be fired in one hand, it could deliver thirty rounds in less than four seconds.

In World War Two, sub-machine guns were used for close combat in confined spaces where firepower counted for more than accuracy. During the battle for the Soviet city of Stalingrad, German soldiers armed with Schmeissers fought from building to building and room to

*An Australian infantry unit practises a **bayonet** charge during training. For direct combat, soldiers had bayonets attached to their rifles so the weapons would double as a spear at close quarters.*

room against Soviet infantry armed with the PPSh-41. The British equivalent was the Sten gun, and American forces used the MIAI Thompson and the M3. All were produced in large numbers. By contrast, the Japanese made only a tiny number of sub-machine guns.

Anti-tank weapons

Another World War Two **innovation** gave infantrymen a fighting chance against armoured vehicles such as tanks. Portable anti-tank weapons fired a special **grenade** that had a front face hollowed out to make a metal-lined cone. When the grenade exploded, it produced a jet of gas and molten metal that could penetrate **armour plating** to a depth of about three times the diameter of the cone. These anti-tank weapons were hazardous to use, however. The British version, the Projector Infantry Anti-Tank (PIAT), was fired by a powerful spring. The **recoil** was supposed to re-set the spring for the next shot, but it often failed to work. The gunner, lying behind the gun, would then have to stand up to reload, exposing himself to enemy fire.

Land-mines, used as anti-tank and anti-vehicle weapons, were horribly dangerous for infantry and **civilians**. They were cases filled with explosives and laid in the ground, where they exploded when disturbed. Their most extensive use was in the deserts of North Africa, where there were few natural barriers and the enemy might attack from any direction. An estimated 18 million unexploded World War Two land-mines remain in Egypt's Western Desert.

*An American soldier keeps watch with a portable anti-tank weapon. The bazooka (seen here), and the similar German panzerfaust, fired **rocket**-propelled grenades. The rocket spewed out flame as it left the barrel, making it dangerous for the user.*

Mobile infantry

German infantry were transported by trucks or vehicles fitted with tracks that enabled them to travel across rough country. The mobility of these forces was demonstrated at the start of Germany's 1941 invasion of the Soviet Union, when the attackers advanced 660 km (410 m) in three weeks. The Allied armies adopted similar measures. Armies also used small, sturdy vehicles for **reconnaissance** and carrying messages. The USA turned out so many four-wheel-drive Jeeps (from 'GPs' or 'general purpose' vehicles) that they became a common mode of transport on all battlefronts.

Artillery

World War One had seen the use of huge heavy guns, or **artillery**, capable of firing **shells** more than 15 kilometres (9 miles). Their attacks on enemy positions were made safely from several kilometres behind the **front lines**. This system was useless against the more mobile targets of World War Two, however. To destroy fast-moving tanks and motorized **infantry**, gunners had to get within visual range. This meant using light artillery pieces that could be moved quickly from place to place.

Mortars are a type of portable artillery used by infantry. Mortars fire shells high rather than far, and so they are effective at close range against enemy positions hidden behind hills or buildings. **Howitzers**, another form of artillery, varied from heavy guns to small, portable versions. The 75 millimetre pack howitzer could break down into parts small enough to be delivered in rough terrain by parachute.

Whether light or heavy, all artillery fired shells of one kind or another. The shells were metal cases containing explosives that caused extensive damage when they exploded on reaching their target. In some cases, the US army used a radio-controlled **fuse** that **detonated** an artillery shell in the air directly above its target, making it up to twenty times more effective than a shell that exploded on or in the ground.

Allied soldiers load shells into an anti-tank gun during the capture of the French town of St Malo in 1944.

The 88

The most famous artillery weapon of World War Two was the German 88 millimetre. Designed as an anti-aircraft gun, the 88 was pressed into service as an anti-tank weapon during the battle for France in 1940. It was also used with great success against Allied tanks in North Africa from 1940 to 1943. The 88 was one of the few weapons that proved effective against Soviet T-34 tanks. From 2000 metres away, a single shell from an 88 could penetrate **armour plating** 100 millimetres thick. While most artillery pieces were in a fixed position between two wheels, the 88 could be smoothly rotated on a platform to fire in any direction.

Self-propelled artillery and rockets

The 88 was light enough to be transported on a truck, but it was not a true mobile weapon. The Germans pioneered self-propelled artillery and it was later taken up by the British and Americans. These weapons were capable of keeping up with tanks, as they were adapted tanks themselves, fitted with high-**velocity** guns. The vehicles, such as the German Jagdtiger which carried a 128 millimetre gun, were heavily armoured to protect the gun crew. Unlike tanks, however, self-propelled artillery had guns that pointed straight ahead, making them vulnerable to attacks from the rear.

The Germans and Soviets also developed battlefield **rocket** launchers that fired gas-propelled missiles armed with explosive **warheads**. The German Nebelwerfer fired six rockets at two-second intervals. Allied troops who encountered it in France called it the 'screaming meanie' for the eerie sound of the incoming rockets.

Rocket launchers were one kind of artillery used in the Battle of Kursk in 1943. The vehicle-mounted Soviet Katyusha, seen here, fired up to 48 rockets from a multiple launcher that was known as a 'Stalin organ'.

Artillery barrages

When a **stalemate** was reached, massed artillery could be used to initiate new assaults. The 900-gun **barrage** with which the British launched the 1942 Battle of El Alamein in North Africa was the heaviest since 1918. During the Battle of Kursk in 1943, 26,000 Soviet artillery pieces fired 42 million **rounds**. In the 1945 Battle for Berlin, the Soviets packed up to 640 guns into each kilometre of their front line. **Civilians** were often victims of artillery barrages. The besieged Soviet citizens of Leningrad endured more than two years of German shelling before the Soviet army relieved the city.

Tanks

In 1941 Germany launched the huge Operation Barbarossa against the Soviet Union. The armoured divisions, including thousands of panzers such as these, led the invasion.

Tanks, with their combination of mobility, powerful guns and thick armour, proved to be the main **offensive** land weapon of World War Two, except in the Far East. Their **caterpillar tracks** enabled them to cross ground impassable by wheeled vehicles. Their guns could rotate to fire **shells** in any direction at enemy tanks or **strongpoints**.

Blitzkrieg

Before the war began, most armies believed that the role of tanks was limited to supporting **infantry** movements. It was the Germans who first adopted the tactic of using tanks backed up by aircraft, **artillery** and infantry to lead all-out assaults.

The invasion of Poland in 1939 was a one-sided contest in which defending infantry stood no chance against Germany's *blitzkrieg*. The Germans' tanks, called panzers, that invaded Poland faced a tougher

test the next year in France, the Netherlands and Belgium. There they were outnumbered by Allied tanks. However, the Allies' tanks were spread out along the entire front. The main panzer force attacked through the hilly, forested land of the Belgian Ardennes, which the French mistakenly thought was impassable by tanks. Bypassing enemy strongpoints, the panzers reached the French coast in eleven days.

That's what I need! That's what I want!
Adolf Hitler after seeing tanks demonstrated in 1933.

Tanks on the Eastern Front

It wasn't until Germany invaded the Soviet Union in 1941 that the panzers met their match. The Soviet T–34 tank had a high-**velocity** gun that could destroy a panzer before the German tank could get in range with its own gun. Its wide tracks enabled it to cross rough or boggy ground that would bring a panzer to a halt. Shells often glanced harmlessly off its sloping **armour plating**.

Panthers and Tigers

The Germans soon incorporated many of the T-34's features in their Panther, widely regarded as the best battle tank of the war. Armed with a 75-millimetre long-range gun, the four-man Panther had armour up to 60 millimetres thick that couldn't be penetrated by the Allies' main anti-tank weapons. Although it weighed 45 tonnes, it had a top speed of 54 kilometres per hour (34 miles per hour).

The Germans also built two giant tanks, the Tiger I and Tiger II, both armed with 88 millimetre guns that could destroy enemy tanks at a range of up to 3 kilometres. The 55-tonne Tiger I was slower than the Panther, and proved most effective in ambushes. The 69-tonne Tiger II was protected by armour up to 180 millimetres thick. One tank commander reported that a Tiger II could take twenty hits without being knocked out.

Japanese tanks

There was little scope for tank warfare in the dense jungles of south-east Asia, where World War Two was also being fought. Japan built only a small number of tanks. Their armour was so thin that American anti-tank shells, which were designed to penetrate much thicker armour, often went right through the tank before exploding.

The versatile tank

The British army used several special-purpose tanks known as 'funnies'. Among them were the flail tank, which exploded mines; the flame-thrower tank, which could project a blast of burning fuel 100 metres; and the bridge-laying and track-laying tanks. For the 1944 invasion of Normandy, the Americans produced an amphibious Sherman tank that floated ashore in an inflatable canvas boat with propellers driven by the tank's engine.

The American Sherman, seen here on the road to Italy in 1944, was the Allies' main battle tank on the Western Front. It was outclassed by the prodigious German Tigers, but so few Tigers were built – only 2000 compared to 30,000 Shermans – that they were overwhelmed by sheer force of numbers.

Fighter planes

A modern air force

The German air force – the Luftwaffe – had officially existed only since 1935. Building the Luftwaffe almost from scratch proved to be an advantage. While many air forces still relied on biplanes (double-winged planes) with bodies partly covered in fabric, the Luftwaffe was equipped with all-metal monoplanes (single-winged planes). In 1937, Germany took the world air speed record with a plane that achieved more than 600 kilometres (370 miles) per hour. This was an early Messerschmitt 109, the fighter which Hitler thought would win control of British skies.

In 1940, Hitler started preparation for an invasion of Britain. For the invasion to succeed, Britain's Royal Air Force (RAF) would have to be destroyed so that it could not protect the British Isles from invasion. The Germans hoped to achieve this with the use of bomber aeroplanes.

Bombers were heavy and slow and needed to be escorted by fighter aircraft. Fighters were lighter and could move fast and turn quickly to fire their guns at approaching enemy planes. A form of combat, known as 'dogfights', had developed between fighter planes during World War One and continued in World War Two. The aircraft would come terrifyingly close to each other to attack and make breathtaking twists and turns to avoid each other's gunfire.

The British fight back

In July 1940, Germany started its air attacks. The two-month onslaught on Britain became known as the Battle of Britain. German bombers

*The two principal fighter planes of the Battle of Britain were the Hawker Hurricane (top) and the Messerschmitt 109 (bottom). The British Hurricane was slower than the German Messerschmitt, but it was more **manoeuvrable**.*

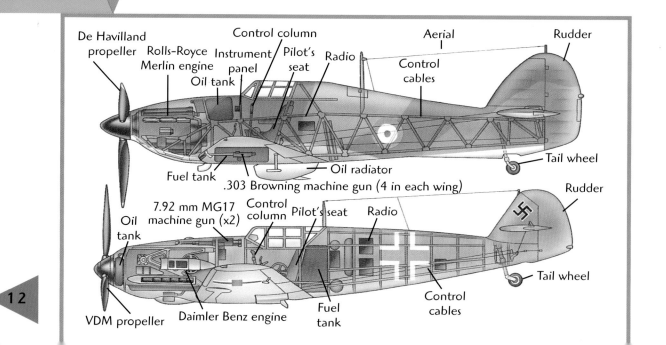

De Havilland propeller
Rolls-Royce Merlin engine
Instrument panel
Oil tank
Control column
Pilot's seat
Radio
Aerial
Control cables
Rudder
Fuel tank
Oil radiator
.303 Browning machine gun (4 in each wing)
Tail wheel

Oil tank
7.92 mm MG17 machine gun (x2)
Control column
Pilot's seat
Radio
Rudder
VDM propeller
Daimler Benz engine
Fuel tank
Control cables
Tail wheel

attacked ships and airfields and, at the beginning of September, began to bomb British cities.

The mainstay of the RAF's fighter wing was the Hawker Hurricane. Adapted from a biplane design, the Hurricane was so sturdy that it could survive damage that would have destroyed most other fighters. Although Hurricanes were credited with 80 per cent of all planes destroyed in the Battle of Britain, they were overshadowed by a new fighter plane, the Supermarine Spitfire. The Messerschmitt 109 was faster and its weapons more powerful, but the Spitfire's tight turns and better handling gave it the edge.

In a huge battle on 15 September, the RAF used all its fighter planes against the massed Luftwaffe forces. The Germans lost 60 aircraft, and two days later Hitler postponed the invasion indefinitely.

Other notable fighters

There were other fighters that were significant to the course of the war. In 1941, the Luftwaffe got the Focke-Wulf 190, another high-speed combat plane. And at the beginning of the war in the Pacific, American fighter pilots were startled to find that their Grumman Wildcats were outclassed by Japan's Mitsubishi Zero.

From 1943 many Allied fighters, such as the Hawker Typhoon, were armed with bombs and **rockets** and used to attack ground targets. The De Havilland Mosquito was one of the most versatile planes of the war. Built of plywood and powered by twin engines, it saw service as a bomber, target-finder, **reconnaissance** plane and night-fighter.

The greatest American contribution to fighter planes in Europe was the P-51 Mustang, seen here behind a group of pilots in Italy in 1944. The Mustang was as fast as the German Focke-Wulf 190, and its 1500-km (900-m) range enabled it to escort American bombers into the heart of Germany.

The first jet

In 1944, when **piston engine technology** had been pushed to its limits, the Luftwaffe introduced the Messerschmitt 262, the first jet aeroplane to see operational service. In a jet engine, the thrust comes from a high-speed stream of hot gases produced by igniting fuel mixed with compressed air. With a top speed of 864 kph (537 mph), the Messerschmitt 262 was in a league of its own. But, by this stage of the war, the Germans had hardly enough fuel to keep their fighters airborne.

Bombers

During the German invasions of Poland and France, Stuka **dive-bombers** proved to be an effective weapon against **infantry**. From September 1940 to May 1941, the Germans also used bombers to mount a campaign, called the Blitz, on London. They also bombed other British cities. But these planes carried a fairly light bomb load and the Germans never developed heavy bombers.

The city of London spreads out below a German Heinkel 111 bomber. The plane was on a raid during the Battle of Britain in 1940.

Mass bombing

It was the British and Americans who adopted the controversial **strategy** of mass bombing with heavy bombers. Air-Marshal 'Bomber' Harris, head of the RAF's Bomber Command, thought that huge, prolonged aerial assaults could destroy Germany's war industry. This would mean attacking targets such as weapons factories, railway centres, and fuel depots.

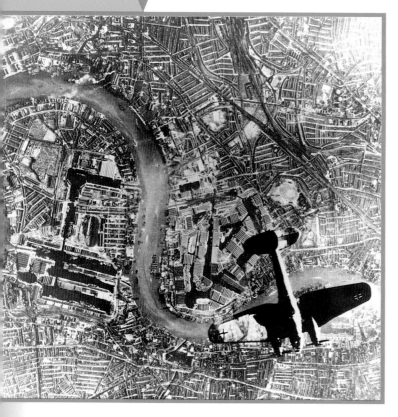

The RAF began its campaign in 1942, when it first flew the Avro Lancaster, a four-engine plane that could carry a bomb load of over 5500 kilograms. Heavy bombers sometimes flew in formations of as many as 1000 aircraft. To reduce the threat from German anti-aircraft defences, the bombers attacked at night. In the dark, however, harassed by fighters and assaulted by **flak**, many bombers missed their intended targets and simply dropped their bombs on any available built-up area.

To improve accuracy, hand-picked RAF crews, known as Pathfinder squadrons, were equipped with advanced navigation systems. Their job was to find the target and mark it with **incendiary bombs** and flares for the main bomber force. Even with the targets marked, the bombs dropped by successive waves of planes tended to creep outside the marked zone. The RAF began to call their strategy 'area bombing'. This term showed there was no distinction being made between industrial and **civilian** targets.

Daylight bombing

The Americans were convinced that precision bombing was possible only in daylight. Their B-24 Liberators and B-17 Flying Fortresses, armed with up to thirteen machine guns, were fitted with Norden bombsights. This device, in theory, enabled the Americans to hit a 30-metre circle from an altitude of 6500 metres. But the bombers proved to be neither as well-protected nor as accurate as had been hoped. During one daylight raid to Germany in August 1943, 60 out of 315 bombers were shot down. It wasn't until long-range P-51 Mustang fighters entered service as escorts for bombers in late 1943 that losses fell to an acceptable level. Even then, fewer than one third of the bombs dropped fell within 300 metres of the specific target.

Bombing from the air was not confined to Europe. On 10 March 1945, American bombers dropped 2000 tonnes of bombs on Tokyo. The resulting **firestorm** destroyed 40 per cent of the city, caused more than 125,000 **casualties** and left over a million people homeless.

Was it worth it?

The Allied bombing campaign diverted about a million German workers into reconstruction work. However, it did not cripple the German war economy until the very end, nor did it destroy civilian morale. The bombing campaign killed more than half a million German civilians. It also took a heavy toll of the attackers. More than 100,000 Allied bomber air crew lost their lives over Germany, the highest casualty rate of any branch of the Western Allies' armed forces.

The bouncing bomb

On the night of 16 May 1943, nineteen Lancaster bombers took off on a raid against three dams that supplied vital hydroelectric power and water to factories in Germany's industrial heartland. The planes carried a special type of 'bouncing bomb' invented by British scientist Barnes Wallis. Released from a height of only 27 metres, the bomb was designed to skip over the water and then slide down the face of the dam before exploding. Two of the dams were damaged, causing floods and subsequent water shortages that affected German industrial production for several months.

The kamikaze was a volunteer corps of suicide bombers in Japan. Their name means 'divine wind', and they were named after a wind that wrecked an invading fleet in the 13th century. The pilots crashed their bomb-laden planes into American ships. Despite their courage, the 1228 pilots who died on their kamikaze missions sank only 34 ships.

Airborne troops

Parachutes were first used as life-saving devices by aircrew forced to abandon their aircraft in mid-air. The parachute slows descent, so that a person hits the ground with a force no greater than if he or she had jumped off a 3-metre wall.

Surprise attacks

The Soviets were the first to realize that airborne troops equipped with parachutes – called paratroops – could be used to mount sudden attacks on targets behind enemy lines. In 1936, the Soviet army defeated an Afghan force by dropping more than 1000 paratroops in a surprise attack. The idea of soldiers attacking from planes also made a deep impression on Hitler. He described a war of the future as 'a sky black with bombers and, leaping from them into the smoke, parachute storm troops, each grasping a machine gun'.

As well as parachuting from planes, German airborne troops pioneered the tactic of landing in **gliders** that were towed behind planes and then released several kilometres from the target. Because the gliders were silent, they could sometimes achieve a degree of surprise denied to parachutists arriving from noisy aeroplanes. They could also deliver weapons and vehicles that were too heavy to be dropped by parachute.

First strikes from the sky

During the 1940 *blitzkrieg*, German glider troops captured the supposedly impregnable Belgian fort of Eben Emael. The next year, German airborne troops led the invasion of Crete. But here they met serious problems. Unlike modern parachutes, which can be steered, the parachutes used in World War Two left their user at the mercy of the wind. Hundreds of German paratroops landed in the sea or got tangled

German parachutists land in Crete in 1941. The white parachutes in the middle are those of the paratroop leaders. Although the Germans eventually captured Crete, 6000 of the invaders were killed or wounded.

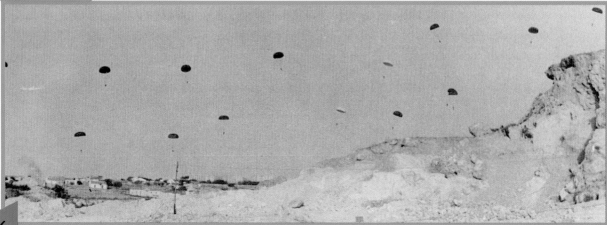

Daring rescue

In 1943 the Italian dictator Benito Mussolini was toppled from power and imprisoned in a mountaintop hotel. Adolf Hitler ordered a force of glider-borne paratroops and **commandos** to rescue his ally. The gliders crash-landed in the hotel grounds, and within minutes Mussolini was bundled into a light plane and carried to freedom. He remained in hiding until 1945, when he was found and executed by communist partisans, or supporters.

in trees. The gliders could not be steered precisely, and many of them flipped over when they made forced landings. After this, Germany made no more large-scale airborne assaults.

The Allies, too, often had problems with airborne operations. When American paratroops and British glider troops spearheaded the 1943 invasion of Sicily, the parachutists ended up scattered all over south-east Sicily, and 70 of the 144 gliders crashed into the sea. It was a similar story when American paratroops were used in the invasion of the Italian mainland at Salerno. One battalion successfully reinforced the Allied invaders. Another, dropped behind German lines, was too dispersed to accomplish its mission of disrupting enemy communications.

British World War Two paratroopers stand by their plane before take-off. World War Two showed the hit-or-miss nature of airborne operations. Many nations continue to use airborne troops, but they rarely parachute into action.

On D-Day, 6 June 1944, when the Allies invaded France from Britain, the paratroopers were the first to arrive. Some lost their lives, landing in trees or in the cold water of the English Channel.

Failed assault

The biggest airborne assault ever was launched in September 1944 by 24,000 British and American paratroops and glider troops. Their objective was to capture key bridges in the German-occupied Netherlands. If they succeeded and held out until advancing ground troops reached them, it would open a way into Germany and might bring a quick end to the war.

The Americans accomplished their tasks, but the British forces landed too far from their main target at Arnhem. By the time they reached the bridge, the Germans had brought in **reinforcements**. Equipment dropped by air fell into enemy hands. After a week's fighting that cost them 7500 **casualties**, the British airborne troops surrendered.

Warships

Mighty battleships

After World War One, it appeared to some that developing air power would spell the end for battleships. Few naval leaders paid attention. Battleships were regarded as almost indestructible, and for naval powers like Britain, Japan and the USA, these mighty vessels were also symbols of national pride.

Weighing more than 35,000 tonnes, battleships were up to 300 metres long and protected by armour as much as 40 centimetres thick. They carried eight or more main guns mounted in **turrets** on the deck. Many of these guns were capable of firing a **shell** weighing about a tonne more than 30 kilometres (19 miles). Battleships also carried dozens of smaller guns, including anti-aircraft guns. Their fuel tanks held over 5000 tonnes of fuel that enabled them to cruise for thousands of kilometres. More than 1000 men were needed to crew one of these ships.

After World War One, Germany had been forbidden to build any warship over about 10,000 tonnes in weight. So the Germans built vessels known as 'pocket battleships', which were, in fact, slightly over the weight limit. The pocket battleships were armed and **armour-plated** like battleships, but were smaller in size. They had advantages, however: they were faster than more heavily-armed real battleships and better armed than smaller, faster warships.

Two damaged battleships burn in Pearl Harbor after the Japanese attack that brought the USA into World War Two.

The Bismarck and the Tirpitz

Allied battleships were positioned in the Atlantic along the routes taken by **convoys** of merchant ships bringing supplies from North America to Britain. Convoys were groups of up to 50 ships travelling together for safety and protected by armed escort ships. The main job of the battleships was to patrol in search of enemy vessels.

Hitler, who knew that German surface ships were no match for British naval power, ordered the construction of two 42,000-tonne battleships, the *Bismarck* and the *Tirpitz*. Their task was to destroy the Atlantic convoys. The *Bismarck* made only one combat voyage. In May 1941, after it blew up a British battlecruiser, the *Bismarck* was sunk by the Allies. The *Tirpitz* never even fought an engagement against warships. In November 1944, the ship was sunk by RAF bombers.

Torpedoes were a type of missile used by ships and by submarines. Launched through water with the power of compressed air, they could travel several thousand metres to explode against a ship's hull.

Battleships in the Pacific

The USA entered World War Two on 8 December 1941, the day after Japanese planes attacked their ships and planes at Pearl Harbor, Hawaii. For the rest of the Pacific war, the USA used its battleships mainly to support **infantry** landings and to protect its aircraft carriers.

Other warships

World War Two warships were designed to fight as a unit, fleet against fleet, with each type of vessel playing a different role. As it turned out, there were few fleet engagements and warships usually operated in small groups or alone.

In order of descending size, cruisers were heavily armed warships that patrolled the oceans at high speed. Destroyers were general-purpose ships, often used to protect larger ships. They were armed with torpedoes as well as guns. Lightly-armed frigates were designed mainly for **reconnaissance**. Both destroyers and frigates were extensively used as convoy escorts.

The Canadians and the British introduced the corvette, a vessel equipped mainly with anti-submarine weapons. Large numbers of minesweepers were deployed to clear the sea lanes of explosive mines. Among other fighting ships were small, very fast patrol boats armed with torpedoes.

Aircraft carriers

In the Pacific, it was not battleships but aircraft carriers that won the war at sea. By the 1930s, aircraft carriers had developed into high-speed floating air bases armed with up to 100 **dive-bombers**, torpedo planes and fighters that could attack targets 800 kilometres (500 miles) away. They heralded a new kind of warfare, in which fleets battled it out without ever coming in sight of each other.

Anatomy of an aircraft carrier

Americans called carriers 'flat tops' because their decks were clear of all obstacles that could interfere with planes taking off and landing. Funnels, masts and the ship's bridge were grouped to one side to maximize the flight deck area. Most of the aircraft were stowed below deck and raised on lifts as required. Carriers were armed with mainly anti-aircraft weapons for defence against attacks from the air. The guns were usually located in bays beneath the flight deck.

The flight deck of a World War Two aircraft carrier as an aeroplane prepares for take-off.

The flight deck – really a floating runway – was high above the water so that planes could operate in stormy seas. The largest carriers were 300 metres long, and so their flight decks were much shorter than a land runway. The aircraft were designed to take off and land at lower speeds and in shorter distances than on shore. During take-off and landing, the carrier sailed full speed into the wind, increasing lift on the aircraft's wings. Planes were also launched with steam-powered catapults that could accelerate a 3-tonne aircraft to more than 100 kilometres per hour (62 miles per hour) in just 17 metres. When they landed, the planes were slowed down by wires strung across the flight deck which hooked into the underside of the aircraft.

Assault on Pearl Harbor

Japan's carrier fleet had been built up as the navy's main strike force by Admiral Isoroku Yamamoto. In their attack on the American base at Pearl Harbor, Japanese warplanes launched from six carriers destroyed or crippled eighteen American warships. The Japanese also destroyed 188 aircraft and damaged another 159. But by chance, all the Americans carriers were at sea on that day. Yamamoto knew that the failure to eliminate them could have serious consequences. 'The sinking of four or five battleships is no cause for celebration,' he wrote.

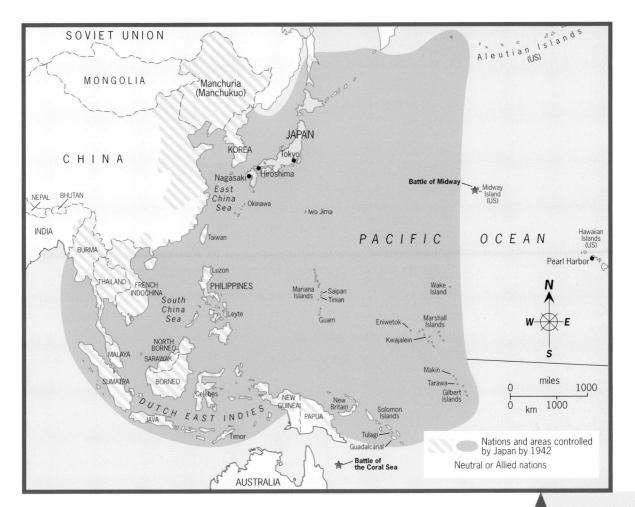

Battles in the Pacific Ocean

The first engagement between carrier fleets came in May 1942, in the Coral Sea north of Australia. One American carrier was sunk and another badly damaged, while one Japanese carrier was destroyed and two damaged. The Americans repaired their damaged carrier within 72 hours, but the Japanese ships remained out of action for months.

By then, Japan had already lost the vital battle for control of the Pacific. Yamamoto knew that Japan could not win a long war against the USA, and planned a bold move to destroy what remained of the American fleet in the Pacific. He would invade Midway, an American-occupied island, and then attack the US fleet when it steamed to the rescue.

What Yamamoto did not know was that the Americans had discovered his intentions by breaking Japan's secret codes. And he mistakenly thought that both US carriers had been sunk in the Coral Sea. On the morning of 4 June 1942, the Japanese found themselves under attack from planes launched from carriers which they had assumed didn't exist. For the loss of one carrier and 150 planes, the Americans destroyed four Japanese carriers and 322 planes. After the Battle of Midway, American task forces gradually imposed their domination on the Pacific.

Until the Americans entered World War Two with their fleet of aircraft carriers, the Japanese had control of a large part of the Pacific islands and nations. The Battle of Midway stopped the Japanese advance and was a turning point in the war.

Amphibious warfare

High-risk operations

One of the riskiest military operations is that of landing troops on heavily-defended coastlines. When Canadian and British troops raided the French port of Dieppe in 1942, more than two-thirds of them were killed, captured or wounded.

Despite the risks involved, the USA had to mount **amphibious** assaults if they were to capture the Pacific islands that led like stepping stones to Japan. To do this they used special assault craft. While warships and aircraft attacked the Japanese defences, the **infantry** raced ashore in landing craft. Timing was critical. If the bombardment stopped too soon, the defenders could slaughter the invaders while they were still in the sea. If the bombardment went on too long, the attackers risked being killed by their own side once they were on land.

Landing craft

The Americans developed several types of landing craft, ranging from small personnel carriers to vessels that could carry tanks and bulldozers, as well as men. Most landing craft were boxy vessels with drawbridge-

The American fleet in the Pacific included cruisers, destroyers, assault craft, and transport vehicles. Many of these vessels can be seen below as troops and supplies are landed on the island of Okinawa during the Allied advance towards Japan.

style bow doors that dropped flat when the craft reached shore so that the attackers could run directly onto the beach. Sometimes, however, the invaders misjudged the depth of the water and the landing craft grounded a long way from the beach, forcing the invaders to wade ashore under heavy fire. That is what happened at the island of Tarawa in 1943, where many landing craft got stuck. The 5000 Japanese defenders inflicted 3000 **casualties** before they were overcome.

The Normandy invasion

The Allies also invaded Italy and North Africa from the sea. However, these assaults were small compared to the huge Operation Neptune,

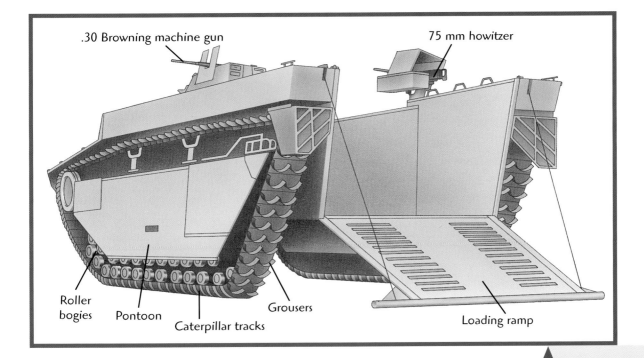

.30 Browning machine gun

75 mm howitzer

Roller bogies

Pontoon

Caterpillar tracks

Grousers

Loading ramp

the naval phase of the invasion of France on 6 June 1944. Neptune called for the landing of 170,000 men in a single day on five beaches along the Normandy coast. An armada of 4000 landing craft, supported by 1000 warships and other vessels, was assembled to put this force ashore. More than 10,000 fighters, bombers and **barrage** balloons provided protection overhead.

Artificial harbours

The Germans didn't know where the invasion would take place, but they were sure that it would be directed against a port. Therefore they concentrated their defences on established harbours. Instead, the Allies brought their own harbours with them in order to land on the beaches they had chosen. The two artificial harbours, called 'Mulberries', were mammoth feats of engineering. More than 200 steel and concrete sections, weighing up to 6000 tonnes each, were used in their construction. There were 33 jetties connected by 16 kilometres (10 miles) of floating roadway. The sections were assembled in dockyards all round Britain and towed to Normandy by 160 tugboats. The Allies also laid an undersea oil pipeline from the Isle of Wight, off the south coast of England.

On the chosen morning, called D-Day, the landing craft were launched up to 20 kilometres (12 miles) from the French coast. More than 130,000 soldiers got ashore in the first sixteen hours, and within ten days, ships were unloading supplies in the artificial harbours. By the end of June, the Allies had landed 850,000 men and 150,000 vehicles on French soil.

After their disastrous landing at Tarawa, the Americans used many more amphibious tractors, known as 'amtracks'. Amtracks had propellers to drive them through the water and **caterpillar tracks** *to carry them over reefs and up onto beaches.*

Submarines

Cutting off supplies

By the summer of 1940, when much of Europe had fallen to the Nazis, Britain was still holding out against Germany. The island nation depended for its survival on supplies shipped from overseas. If this lifeline could be cut, Britain would be forced to surrender. In a series of attacks known as the Battle of the Atlantic, Germany tried to starve Britain into submission by attacking merchant ships from beneath the waves.

Germany's main weapon was a submarine. The Type VII U-boat was driven by diesel engines on the surface and by a battery-powered motor under water. U-boats lay in wait along the routes taken by **convoys**. They could detect targets by picking up the sound of propellers with an underwater microphone called a hydrophone. The U-boats usually approached under the surface, using a **periscope** to keep the ship in view. Once the target was in range, the U-boat fired at it with torpedoes. If there were warships nearby, the U-boat then dived deeper to make its escape. A U-boat could descend to 200 metres and stay submerged for many hours before surfacing for air and to recharge its batteries.

Heavy losses

To maximize their effectiveness, U-boats were organized into groups known as 'wolf-packs'. When a U-boat captain sighted a convoy, he would communicate its position and shadow it until the rest of the pack closed in for the kill. U-boats inflicted heavy losses on convoys in the Atlantic: in one attack on a convoy in 1942, a wolf pack sank 22 out of 103 ships.

The hunters become the hunted

The attacks continued successfully into the spring of 1943. Then, Allied shipping losses suddenly dropped while U-boat losses mounted sharply. There were several reasons for this reversal. More convoy escort ships were built and fitted with new detection systems. The development of longer-range aircraft meant the Allies could patrol further out into the

A surfaced U-boat under attack by Allied aircraft during the Battle of the Atlantic.

Atlantic. And British code-breakers had broken the U-boat radio communications code. By reading enemy messages, the Allies could route convoys out of harm's way and hunt down U-boats that had given away their positions. Germany had, briefly, come close to defeating Britain with its U-boats, but at a heavy cost: 28,000 of the 40,000 men who served in U-boats were killed.

The American submarine force

After the Japanese attack on Pearl Harbor, the US Navy entered World War Two in 1941 with only 14 working submarines in the Pacific. During the war, another 130 arrived from American shipyards. The USA used these in long-range attacks in Japanese-controlled Pacific waters.

Anti-submarine weapons and submarine tracking devices

Depth-charges were underwater bombs. Explosive-packed steel drums, they were set to go off at a certain depth when dropped near their targets.

Hedgehogs fired small bombs from warships, such as destroyers or corvettes. The bombs were fired ahead of the vessels. This was a more effective way of attacking a submarine than with depth-charges, which were discharged after the ship had passed over a U-boat. Unlike depth-charges, the bombs exploded only on contact with a U-boat.

Asdic (an early form of **sonar**) stood for Anti-Submarine Detection Investigation Committee. It sent out sound waves to detect and locate submarines. If the sound waves struck a U-boat, they were reflected to a receiver and transmitted as a loud 'ping'. This is called echolocation.

Huff-duff (high-frequency direction finder) tuned in to U-boat radio transmissions. When two or more Huff-duff stations picked up a U-boat signal, the submarine's approximate position could be plotted.

Microwave radar was a type of **radar** (radio detection and ranging) operating on very short wavelengths. Unlike long-wave radar, microwave radar signals could not be detected by U-boats.

A view of a sinking Japanese ship from the periscope of an American submarine. The United States' submarines accounted for two-thirds of Japan's merchant shipping losses and about one-third of its naval losses. They sank one battleship, eleven cruisers and eight aircraft carriers, including the 71,000-tonne Shinano, the largest vessel to be sunk in the war.

Radar

One of many British radar stations that helped pinpoint incoming enemy aircraft during the Battle of Britain. The British were quick to develop radar and this gave them an early advantage.

A new detection device

Before World War Two, people believed that 'the bomber will always get through'. That they didn't is largely due to **radar**, a system for detecting and locating objects. Developed in the 1930s, radar works by bouncing a radio beam off a metallic object such as an aircraft or ship. By measuring the time taken for the echo to reach a receiver, the radar operator can estimate the range and course of the plane or ship. Radar also enables pilots to navigate at night. Although radar served all of the armed forces, it was the air war that accelerated its development.

The British advantage

Britain quickly recognized the importance of radar. When the Battle of Britain began, the RAF had a chain of radar stations that could detect enemy aeroplanes and direct Allied fighters to engage them. With this early-warning system, RAF interceptors could take off at the last possible minute and therefore their fuel supplies would outlast those of the German fighters. The Germans underestimated the value of the British radar system and made no systematic effort to destroy it.

The British secretly developed a miniature airborne radar set. In November 1940, a radar-equipped Bristol Beaufighter shot down a German bomber at night. To explain the success without giving away the radar secret, the RAF claimed that its night-fighter crews were selected from pilots with exceptional eyesight who were fed on a diet rich in carrots (which were said to improve vision).

Countermeasures

By the time the Allies began their mass bombing campaign, Germany had set up its own radar stations. The Germans had one radar plotting an incoming bomber's course and another directing a night-fighter towards the attacker. The British learned how to **jam** the signals to the German stations, but Germany quickly fitted its night-fighters with radar sets that enabled them to find targets without any input from the ground.

Devious devices

The British developed many countermeasures against German air defences. MANDREL was a jamming device against the German early-warning radar system. TINSEL **amplified** the sound of a bomber's engines to drown out the German fighters' radio communications. BOOZER was a set carried in the bomber to warn the pilot when he had been detected by enemy radar.

Cat and mouse over Germany

In late 1942, the RAF introduced a remote navigation system code-named OBOE, which used two radar stations about 160 kilometres (100 miles) apart. One station, called 'cat', directed a bomber by radar pulses. The other station, called 'mouse', signalled the aircraft to drop its bombs when it reached its target. But OBOE's range was limited and it could direct only one aircraft at a time. Early in 1943, a better system was found. British and American bombers were equipped with H2S, a radar set that could 'map' the ground even under cloud and pick out targets up to 40 kilometres (25 miles) ahead.

The Germans then developed airborne radar sets which enabled their fighters to home in on H2S signals. But the British countered once again with WINDOW, a method of confusing enemy radar systems by dropping aluminium strips that reflected radar beams. This technique was first used in raids on Hamburg, Germany, in the summer of 1943. As the RAF planes made their bombing runs, the crews heaved bundles of WINDOW strips out of the aircraft. On the German radar screens, the blips of the bombers were lost in what appeared to be a heavy snowstorm.

*Radar was used not just in the air, but for sea operations, too. In this operations room in the dungeons of Dover Castle on the British coast, radar information was gathered and used to direct coastal **artillery** in attacks on enemy ships.*

Communications

Radio operators on a French ship listen out for signals of distress from other ships.

New developments in radio **technology** transformed communications on the World War Two battlefield. Radios did not require cables, as field telephones and the **telegraph** had done in World War One. Instead, radio messages and signals were transmitted through the air without the use of wires. By bouncing signals off a layer of the atmosphere called the ionosphere, messages were transmitted over the airwaves hundreds or even thousands of kilometres. Radio communication was vital to all branches of the armed forces, but its greatest impact was felt by the ground forces. In World War One, army commanders had often been left helpless spectators of the battles they were supposed to be directing. In World War Two, the instant communication provided by radios gave them important advantages. Commanders could now respond immediately to control troop movements, call up **reinforcements** or air support, and direct **artillery** fire.

Leading from the front

Radio was not new, but radio sets had become more portable since World War One. Compact **electronic** devices called **vacuum tubes** were used to **amplify** radio signals, making it possible to build radio sets small enough to be carried by a single man.

Some generals took advantage of the new **technology** to command battles from close to the **front line**, rather than from headquarters in the rear. General Hans Guderian, Germany's leading *blitzkrieg* commander, who had served as a signals officer in World War One, kept up with his troops in a radio-equipped command vehicle. The American general, George Patton, used radio to lead from the front. Patton said that armies were like a piece of spaghetti: you couldn't push a piece of spaghetti, you had to pull it. The British commander Bernard Montgomery used radio broadcasts to boost the morale of his troops. He became the first general in history to broadcast directly to his forces.

All German tanks were equipped with radio, which enabled them to co-ordinate their movements. Panzer tanks often defeated larger Soviet armoured forces because of this advantage. Only the Soviet commanders' vehicles were fitted with radio and instructions to the rest of the tank unit were passed on by crewmen waving signal flags. German tank crews could recognize the Soviet command vehicle by its aerial and always tried to destroy it first. If the command vehicle was knocked out, the rest of the unit, lacking clear instructions about what to do next, often became confused and demoralized.

Clear signal

The German army, however, used low-frequency AM (amplitude modulation) radio, which suffers from atmospheric interference and can easily be **jammed**. The Americans used high-frequency FM (frequency modulation) radio, an American invention of the 1930s. FM eliminated interference to produce a signal much clearer than AM, and was difficult to jam. The value that the US forces attached to communications was shown in the strength of their Signal Corps, the men and women who installed, operated and maintained the communications equipment. It grew from 27,000 at the war's outset to about 350,000 by war's end.

The USA had the best communications equipment in World War Two. This American mortar crew could remain in constant touch with its commander or headquarters through its portable radio.

Soldiers used radio to get news from the outside world as well as for communication. These Germans, cut off in their underground living quarters, tune in to a radio broadcast.

The code-breakers

These German signal troops are using an Enigma machine, although the official description at the time was a 'teletype'. The Allies managed to keep their seizure of an Enigma machine a secret, and the Germans went on using Enigma codes until the end of the war.

During World War Two, radio transmissions were often intercepted by the enemy. Because of this, important radio messages were sent in codes, or secret symbols or words. Each side in the war eavesdropped on the other and used **cryptanalysts** to try and crack the secrets of their enemies' codes.

Enigma

The Germans invented what they thought was an unbreakable secret code based on an encoding machine called Enigma. (Enigma means 'mystery'.) The machine resembled a typewriter, with a keyboard and a panel of individually lettered lamps. When the operator pressed a key, one of the letters lit up. The process also worked in reverse, so that if pressing key B produced the letter K, pressing key K produced the letter B. This produced a message that was unreadable unless the person at the other end also had an Enigma machine.

The Enigma message was then transmitted by radio in Morse code. (This international code sends messages using a pattern of short and long noises or flashes to represent letters of the alphabet.) A radio operator receiving an Enigma message in Morse turned it into letters and then typed it out on another Enigma machine to produce the original message. The Enigma machine had billions of possible settings, which were changed daily so that the enemy would never get a chance to catch up and break the code. The weakness of the system was that the sender had to let the receiver know which setting to use.

British cryptanalysts used a kind of **electromechanical** computer called a Bombe to find settings that would turn

an Enigma message into plain German. Their job was made much easier after May 1941, when a British destroyer seized an Enigma machine and a list of settings from a crippled U-boat. Within a week, the cryptanalysts had cracked the German U-boat code. There were occasional setbacks when the Germans upgraded their Enigma machines, but the Allied code-breakers could often read U-boat signals within hours of their interception.

A code-cracking computer

The Germans used another code, called Fish, which was even more complex than the Enigma codes. To crack it, British scientists developed the first **electronic** computer, Colossus, which could test messages at the rate of 5000 characters a second. It helped decipher German messages showing that Hitler believed the Allied invasion of France would take place near Calais rather than in Normandy.

Japan's open secrets

The Japanese also developed a navy code that they believed was unbreakable. In fact, the Americans cracked it within four months. It was thanks to the code-breakers that US forces uncovered Admiral Yamamoto's plan for the attack on Midway Island. In April 1943, American code-breakers decrypted a message revealing that Admiral Yamamoto would be flying to the island of Bougainville. When the admiral arrived, a force of P-38 fighters intercepted his plane and shot it out of the sky.

The ability to read Japanese naval codes meant that the Americans knew the whereabouts of Japan's warships for most of the Pacific war. Their lack of secure codes probably cost Japan a third of their shipping fleet.

Before the invention of computers made the task easier, de-coding enemy messages in World War Two was done by people on manual decoders such as this one. It was a laborious process of trial and error. A computer did the same thing but thousands of times faster.

Navajo code

The US Marine Corps in the Pacific used a simple, but effective, voice code. Navajo Native Americans serving with the Marines transmitted messages in their complex, unwritten language. This was understood by only a handful of non-Navajos. The Japanese never succeeded in breaking this minority language 'code'.

The propaganda weapon

UNITED
we are strong

UNITED we will win

Propaganda was often direct and simple, designed to inspire loyalty and build support for the war effort. This poster encourages civilians to trust that the united efforts and weapons of the Allies would win the war.

Warring nations have always used propaganda to raise the morale of their citizens and dishearten their enemies. In World War Two, radio and film **technology** offered increased opportunities for manipulating the attitudes of **civilians**. Propaganda was aimed at civilians both at home and abroad. On both sides, radio broadcasts were made to enemy nations with the aim of undermining loyalty, changing opinions and sowing seeds of doubt. On the other hand, cinema audiences flocked to films glorifying the efforts of brave men and women in their armed forces.

Everywhere, posters exhorted citizens to do their bit, maintain security and support their country's efforts. Aircraft made it possible to distribute printed propaganda in enemy territory as well. For the first few months of the war, British bombers dropped millions of propaganda leaflets on Germany.

Radio propaganda

As the Nazi Minister for Public Enlightenment and Propaganda, Josef Goebbels was in complete control of the German press and radio. He encouraged German citizens to buy cheap, mass-produced radio sets that could only receive German stations. When war broke out, 70 per cent of German households had radios, the highest percentage in the world. Compulsory listening was introduced, and loudspeakers were installed in factories. Listening to any non-German controlled station was a crime punishable by death.

In nations where the media was not under complete state control, there was still censorship (banning of certain information) in wartime. British and American radio stations censored programmes which they thought might breach security or damage morale. They tended to exaggerate victories and play down defeats, but in general told the truth.

British Prime Minister Winston Churchill and US President Franklin D Roosevelt used radio to speak directly to the people. Churchill stirred his listeners with rousing speeches that did not flinch from giving bad news. Roosevelt adopted a reassuring tone in his regular 'fireside chats'. By contrast, Hitler rarely addressed the German public after 1942. Goebbels was forced to build up a picture of the Nazi leader as a man working night and day to save Germany.

Germany's minister of propaganda Josef Goebbels makes a radio broadcast during World War Two. Goebbels believed that radio was the most important means of influencing the population.

Propaganda of death

The Nazis whipped up hatred against Jews so that few people would object when the government stripped the Jews of their property and legal rights. Goebbels came up with slogans such as, 'The Jews are our misfortune.' Julius Streicher, a publisher who was executed after the war for his 'propaganda of death', filled the pages of his newspaper with obscene caricatures of Jews.

Hitler used the cover of war to carry out his 'final solution'. This meant the murder of all Jews in German-occupied territories. In a kind of reverse propaganda, any mention of this **genocide** was forbidden. Although there were rumours, the terrible truth was not uncovered until the war ended.

Japanese propaganda

The Japanese propaganda effort was aimed at persuading the people of south-east Asia that Japan was liberating them from colonial powers. At home, the Japanese were kept in ignorance of the course of the war. Defeats were hushed up. After the Battle of Midway, the wounded Japanese sailors were brought ashore at night in secret and treated in isolation wards. Even Japanese politicians were not told of the disaster.

Famous propagandists

Radio propaganda was used to lower enemy morale. One famous figure, Tokyo Rose (actually an American named Iva Togori D'Aquino) broadcast a daily programme from Japan heard by American servicemen in the Pacific. She was later arrested for treason. Lord Haw-Haw, who broadcast throughout the war from Germany to the UK, was also an American, William Joyce. He had lived in England for much of his life and was a fascist. In his radio programme, Joyce spouted Nazi propaganda in an upper-class British accent. After the war, Joyce was hanged for treason.

The home front

Right from the start, the Allies committed all their human and industrial resources to the war effort. Factories switched from the production of peacetime products, such as cars, to wartime necessities, such as aircraft and ships. They operated around the clock, and women were drafted into the workforce.

On the US **home front**, aircraft production rose from below 6000 in 1941 to more than 96,000 in 1945 thanks to the improved techniques and the influx of women workers. Shipbuilding also boomed. Using mass-production methods, the United States launched 140 freighters a month in 1943. These vessels, called Liberty ships, were constructed to a standardized design with prefabricated sections. One Liberty ship was built in only 80 hours, 30 minutes. The USA was able to supply not only its own military needs, but also provided more than one-quarter of Britain's and the Soviet Union's.

Germany's folly

Compared to the combined industrial muscle of the Allies, the Nazis were slow to introduce an all-out war effort. Until 1941, Germany's factories operated much as they had in peacetime. Production of ordinary domestic products actually rose. Hitler had promised a quick victory and was reluctant to admit that the war might drag on for years. He refused to allow women to join the labour force. Their job, said his propaganda chief Josef Goebbels, was 'being beautiful and having children'.

A trainee welder works on the construction of a Liberty ship. Six million women workers helped double industrial output in the United States during World War Two.

> War is won in the factories.
>
> Soviet leader Josef Stalin.

Forced labour

As the war continued, Nazi Germany tried to solve its manpower problem by using Jews and other prisoners of war as forced labour. Many of these workers were fed on starvation rations, housed in appalling conditions and denied medical care. The Nazis tried to justify this treatment by claiming that Jews and Soviets were sub-human. But in 1943, the Soviet Union – where women made up more than half the labour force – produced twice as many armoured fighting vehicles as Germany did.

Japan's ruin

Japan didn't have the raw materials to fight a long war. All of its oil and most of its steel had to be imported. The nation had survived at the beginning of the war by plundering the nations it had conquered in the Pacific. But once the Allies won control of the Pacific Ocean, Japan was doomed.

SAVE YOUR CANS
Help pass the Ammunition

M°CLELLAND BARCLAY USNR.

PREPARE YOUR TIN CANS
FOR WAR
1 REMOVE TOPS AND BOTTOMS
2 TAKE OFF PAPER LABELS
3 WASH THOROUGHLY
4 FLATTEN FIRMLY

*A US poster encourages **civilians** to save scrap metal that can be recycled to make weapons and **ammunition**.*

A factory produces synthetic rubber gas masks used to protect soldiers and civilians against poisonous gas attacks.

Synthetic rubber and fuel

In 1939, the USA used half of all the world's natural rubber. Ninety per cent of the rubber came from countries that were occupied by the Japanese. When supplies dried up, the Americans launched a crash programme to develop a synthetic substitute. By 1945, the United States was producing nearly a million tonnes of synthetic rubber a year.

Germany had to import most of its fuel oil. When supplies were cut off by the advancing Soviet army, the Germans began producing synthetic fuel from coal. In 1945, 85 per cent of the fuel used by German aircraft was synthetic, but there simply wasn't enough to keep the planes flying.

Rockets and guided missiles

Hitler's wonder weapons

In the summer of 1944, as the Allies closed in on Germany, Hitler launched his 'wonder weapons', the V-1 and V-2. (The V stood for *vergeltung* or 'reprisal'.) The V-1 (dubbed the 'buzz bomb' or 'doodlebug' by Londoners) was really a jet-propelled pilotless aircraft, rather than a **rocket**. It carried an 850-kilogram **warhead** and had a range of about 250 kilometres (155 miles). The V-1's course was preset and regulated by an autopilot, a magnetic compass and a propeller-driven distance counter. When the set distance was reached, the engine's fuel supply cut off and the V-1 plunged to the ground. Once the engine stopped, people on the ground knew they had only about fifteen seconds to reach shelter.

Fighting the V-1 menace

More than 10,000 V-1s were launched by the Germans against Britain before the Allies overran their launch sites in France. Altogether, nearly 2500 V-1s hit London. They killed more than 6000 people, injured 17,000 and damaged about 23,000 homes. Although they were not particularly reliable or accurate, V-1s were cheaper to make than aeroplanes and did more damage than German bombers had in the Battle of Britain.

The flying bombs were fairly slow and flew on fixed courses at low altitudes. Because of this, they could be intercepted by fighters, including Britain's first jet, the Gloster Meteor. Since there was a risk of fighters blowing themselves up if they **detonated** the warheads at too close a range, pilots learned how to nudge the V-1s onto courses that would make them crash harmlessly in thinly populated areas.

Allied anti-aircraft guns had little success against the V-1s until they began using a **radar**-guided

Allied airmen examine parts of a V–2 rocket that fell in Belgium. About 3000 V–2s were fired by the Germans in World War Two.

system. This was coupled with an **electronic** aiming device which automatically adjusted itself to the V-1's course and speed – it could aim a **shell** at a position in the sky where the V-1 would be when the shell arrived. Radio-controlled **fuses** then detonated the shells when they came within range of their target. The combination of these three devices worked so well that in the last major V-1 attack, only four of the ninety-four missiles launched got through.

The V-2

There was no defence against the V-2, a liquid-fuelled rocket which rose 80 kilometres (50 miles) into the sky and descended at 5000 kilometres per hour (3100 miles per hour). It exploded before its victims heard its sonic boom.

After Germany surrendered, both the USA and the Soviet Union used V-2 scientists to develop their own rocket programmes. Wernher von Braun, seen here at an American rocket launch, oversaw the development of intercontinental ballistic missiles and the rockets that would take American astronauts to the Moon in 1969.

The V-2 was designed by rocket engineer Wernher von Braun and was Germany's biggest weapons project. Its production employed 20,000 people, mainly slave labourers. The problem with the V-2 was its expense. It cost 50 times as much to make as a V-1, yet carried a warhead that was only slightly bigger.

If Germany had developed its V weapons a few months earlier, it is possible that they might have delayed the Allied invasion of France. In the event, the weapons came too late to affect the course of the war. But their deadly potential was not lost on military strategists and scientists. The V-1 was one of the first long-range, **guided missiles**. The unstoppable V-2, with its high **trajectory** and **supersonic** descent, was an early **ballistic missile**. Both represented significant steps in the development of weapons of the future.

The atomic bomb

Two days before the outbreak of World War Two, the Danish scientist Niels Bohr published an article outlining the theory of nuclear energy. If an atom of a heavy **element**, such as uranium or plutonium, is split, the energy released can produce an explosion of colossal power. When Bohr discovered that German scientists had found a method of splitting uranium, he contacted the German-born Jewish physicist Albert Einstein, who had settled in the United States when Hitler came to power. Einstein wrote to President Roosevelt, warning him that the Nazis might develop a type of nuclear weapon called an atomic bomb.

Race to build the bomb

Einstein's warning resulted in what was then the largest enterprise in the history of science. A $2 billion programme to make the first nuclear weapon crammed about thirty years of **technological** development into under five years. Code-named the Manhattan Project, the USA's race to build the bomb employed more than 40,000 people at 37 secret installations across the United States and Canada. The largest site was at Oak Ridge, Tennessee, where a plant was built to process uranium. Plutonium was produced at Hanford in the state of Washington.

The atomic bomb was tested only once, on 16 July 1945, when a piece of plutonium the size of a tennis ball exploded in the New Mexico desert with a blast equivalent to 20,000 tonnes of conventional explosives.

The actual design and building of the uranium and plutonium bombs took place at Los Alamos, New Mexico, under the direction of the American physicist J Robert Oppenheimer. Many of the scientists recruited by Oppenheimer were German-Jewish exiles driven from Germany by Hitler's anti-Jewish policies. Germany still had scientists who were capable of developing a bomb, but Hitler was not interested in doing so. He scornfully dismissed nuclear weapons as 'Jewish physics'.

The Manhattan Project therefore turned out to be a race with only one competitor. There were many hurdles. One of the biggest was how to make a 'trigger' that would make the nuclear material explode with maximum release of energy. Eventually the scientists came up with two methods. For uranium, one mass of uranium was fired at terrific **velocity** at another mass of uranium. For plutonium, the nuclear material was

A Japanese mother and son sit inside a shack where their house used to be. They built the shack out of the wreckage left after the atomic bomb was dropped on Nagasaki.

packed in explosives which, when **detonated**, concentrated the plutonium so that the entire mass exploded almost instantaneously. The USA now had its nuclear weapons.

The decision to drop the bomb

By the summer of 1945, Germany had been defeated but Japan continued to fight the Allies in the Pacific. The Americans were considering an invasion of Japan, which they reckoned would cost them as many as 250,000 **casualties**.

Instead, US President Harry Truman (who had taken over on Roosevelt's death) ordered the terrible new weapon to be deployed. On 6 August 1945, a B-29 Superfortress plane dropped a uranium atomic bomb on the Japanese city of Hiroshima. It killed 80,000 **civilians** in seconds. Three days later, a plutonium atomic bomb was detonated over Japan at Nagasaki, a city of 212,000 people. The bomb immediately killed one-third of the population and injured a further 77,000. In both cities, more than twice as many victims died later, from **radiation sickness**. One week later, on 14 August 1945, Japan surrendered. World War Two was over.

> *The unleashed power of the atom has changed everything save our modes of thinking and we thus drift towards unparalleled catastrophe.*
>
> Albert Einstein on the significance of the atom bomb. Einstein knew that human beings now had immense power for destruction but perhaps not the wisdom to control this power.

Medicine

There were no medical defences against the devastation of **radiation**, but generally the wounded of World War Two had a better chance of survival than in any previous conflict. The death rate among hospitalized American soldiers fell to only four per cent from fifty per cent a hundred years earlier. The reasons for this improvement were new drugs, better surgical techniques and the use of motorized ambulances and planes. In the Allied campaign that followed the invasion of France, over 100,000 **casualties** were **evacuated** by air.

A wounded US Marine on the island of Tarawa in the Pacific is given plasma to replace lost blood. The new method of separating and storing plasma saved many lives in World War Two.

Plasma

Blood **transfusions** had saved the lives of many World War One soldiers suffering from heavy blood loss. But the problem with blood is that, even when refrigerated, it deteriorates within two days. In 1938, Dr Charles Drew, an American transfusion specialist, discovered that by separating plasma (the liquid part of blood) from the blood cells and then refrigerating them separately, they could be recombined up to a week later for a transfusion.

Drew also discovered that plasma, unlike whole blood, could be given to anyone regardless of their blood type. Plasma-only transfusions were good for treating World War Two burn victims who lost a lot of fluid but few blood cells. Other researchers discovered how to increase the shelf life of plasma by freeze-drying it and sealing it in plastic bags. When it was needed for a transfusion, the dried plasma was simply mixed with sterile water.

Anti-bacterial drugs

Sulfanilamide, an **anti-bacterial** drug first used in 1936, was issued to troops in both the Allied and German armies. Every soldier carried a first aid pack containing a package of sulfa powder which was dusted onto open wounds. Sulfanilamide saved the lives of many Allied soldiers fighting in the jungles of south-east Asia, where even minor wounds quickly became infected if left untreated.

DDT

Insects transmitted a number of diseases, such as typhus, which were major killers in the conflicts before World War Two. DDT, the first synthetic chemical **insecticide**, was mass-produced from 1939. When US troops captured Naples in Italy in 1943, they discovered that typhus had broken out. They prevented an **epidemic** by dusting almost the whole population with DDT powder. The Americans also virtually eradicated malaria in Italy by spraying swampland with the chemical. DDT was called a 'saviour of mankind' when it was introduced. However, it was banned by many countries in the 1970s after scientists discovered that it built up in the food-chain, poisoning insect-eating animals and their predators.

The first antibiotic

A huge breakthrough in the treatment of infection with **antibiotics** occurred during World War Two. Penicillin had been discovered in 1928 by the Scottish bacteriologist Alexander Fleming, who obtained it from certain types of mould. Although Fleming demonstrated that penicillin had remarkable anti-bacterial properties, he could not produce it in useful quantities. When war broke out, British scientists asked American scientists to help. It took three years to find a way to mass-produce penicillin, but it was available when Allied forces launched the D-Day invasion in 1944.

Fighting malaria

In the Far East, malaria transmitted by mosquito bites killed more soldiers than bombs or bullets did. Even when malaria was not fatal, it caused a fever that made soldiers too ill to fight. Malaria hospitalized more than half of the British Commonwealth soldiers serving in Burma in 1942. By 1945 the use of anti-malarial drugs, such as **quinine,** had cut the sickness rate by more than 90 per cent. The Americans used a synthetic anti-malarial drug called Atabrine. It had unpleasant side effects, including headaches and nausea. Medics watched over servicemen at meal times, making sure that each man swallowed his dose before he was allowed to eat.

Penicillin goes into mass production. Workers on an assembly line prepare vials of the much-needed antibiotic for packing and shipping to the battlefronts.

A scientific revolution

The nature of the weapons and the advances in **technology** in World War Two helped to make it the most lethal conflict in history. Over 50 million people died during the war. More than half of these people were **civilians**.

War changes science

The most important technological developments were **radar**, the **electronic** computer, the **ballistic missile** and the atomic bomb. These were the work of teams of scientists, and their success changed the way in which science was conducted. Before the war, most scientific advances were made by individuals or small groups following their own lines of research. After World War Two, government and industry became the main employers of scientists. In a sense, World War Two was the time in which science, until then seen as a force for good, lost its innocence.

The nuclear age

The atomic bombs that exploded over Japan in 1945 cast a shadow that still hasn't lifted. In 1949 the Soviet Union tested its own atomic bomb, an action that started a nuclear weapons race with the USA. In the late 1950s, nuclear **warheads** were fitted to long-range missiles based on the design of Germany's V-2 **rocket**. These exposed everybody on the planet to the risk of nuclear attack. In the 1960s, the Americans installed nuclear missiles on submarines, the design of which owed a lot to German U-boats.

A descendant of World War Two weapons, this air defence system has a multiple launcher holding four lethal missiles. The launcher is positioned between a radar and an optical tracker system.

The threat of mutual destruction has deterred world powers from using nuclear weapons. But dozens of wars have been fought with other weapons developed or improved in World War Two. By the outbreak of the Korean War in 1950, jet fighters had largely replaced **piston engine** warplanes. In the 1991 Gulf War, the USA attacked Iraqi targets with cruise missiles, a high-technology development from Germany's V-1s. Tanks and other armoured fighting vehicles remain the main **offensive** weapons of land warfare.

Weapons systems

World War Two marked the beginning of the evolution of weapons into high-tech 'weapons systems'. A modern battle tank, for example, bristles with offensive and defensive devices. These include communications equipment, target-detecting sensors, computer-guided and **laser-**guided aiming devices, and equipment to protect the crew from attack by chemical or biological weapons.

Everyday technology

Much of the technology developed for World War Two military purposes has been adapted to peacetime use. Nuclear power has been harnessed to provide energy. The jet engine has made it possible for travellers to fly swiftly around the world. Radar technology means these journeys can be made safely even when visibility is poor, and by night as well as day. Electronic computers have become standard tools for communication and processing information. The USA's synthetic rubber programme laid the foundations of the modern plastics industry. **Antibiotics** have saved countless lives. **Insecticides** have reduced disease and boosted crop yields, although at a cost to the environment.

This B–2 plane can carry nearly 20 tonnes of nuclear or non-nuclear weapons on long-range missions. It is called a 'stealthy' aircraft because it is hard to detect by radar due to its shape and construction.

Timeline

1928	Discovery of penicillin
1931	Development of radar begins in Britain
1933	Hitler comes to power in Germany
1935	26 February: Radar successfully tested
1936	First use (by Soviet Union) of parachutes to attack behind enemy lines
	First use of sulfanimide as anti-bacterial drug
1937	Messerschmitt 109 takes world air speed record
1938	Charles Drew successfully separates blood plasma from blood cells and stores for transfusions
1939	Mass production of DDT begins
	29 August: Soviet Union signs non-aggression pact with Germany
	1 September: Germany invades Poland
	3 September: Britain and France declare war on Germany
1940	First use of German 88 mm as anti-tank weapon
	First use of airborne radar set
	10 May: Germany invades Denmark, Norway, Belgium, the Netherlands and France
	10 June: Italy declares war on France and Britain
	July–September: Battle of Britain
	27 September: Tripartite Pact signed by Japan, Germany and Italy
1941	First use of Focke-Wulf 190 by Luftwaffe
	May: British seize German Enigma machine and code-book
	20 May: Germany invades Crete
	27 May: Sinking of German battleship *Bismarck*
	22 June: Germany invades Soviet Union in Operation Barbarossa
	9 October: Commencement of Manhattan Project approved by President Roosevelt
	7 December: Japan attacks Pearl Harbor
1942	OBOE (remote radar navigation system) introduced by RAF
	March: Start of heavy bombing campaign by RAF against Germany
	6–8 May: Battle of the Coral Sea
	4 June: Battle of Midway
	1 September–February 1943: Battle for Stalingrad
	23 October: Battle of El Alamein
1943	H2S (airborne radar navigation system) introduced by RAF
	WINDOW (anti-radar system) introduced by RAF
	July–August: Battle of Kursk
	10 July: Allies invade Sicily
1944	First use of Messerschmitt 262 jet aeroplane by Luftwaffe
	6 June: Allied invasion of Normandy coast in Operation Neptune (D-Day)
	12 June: First V-1s hit London
	8 September: First V-2s hit London
1945	10 March: USA drops 2000 tonnes of bombs on Tokyo
	April: Battle for Berlin
	7 May: Germany surrenders to Allies
	16 July: First atomic bomb tested (in New Mexico, USA)
	6 August: USA drops atomic bomb on Hiroshima
	9 August: USA drops atomic bomb on Nagasaki
	14 September: Japan agrees to unconditional surrender to Allies, ending World War Two
1949	Soviet Union tests its first atomic bomb

Further reading and places of interest

Further reading

Books

Non-fiction

History of Britain: The Blitz, Andrew Langley, Heinemann Library, 1995
Ultimate Aircraft, Philip Jarrett, Dorling Kindersley, 2000
World War II Aircraft, Jeffery L Ethell, Collins/Jane's, 1995
World War II Warships, Bernard Ireland, Collins/Jane's, 1999
Tanks: Look Inside: Cross-Sections, Richard Chasemore and Ian Harvey,
    Dorling-Kindersley, 1996
The Home Front: Women's War, Fiona Reynoldson, Wayland, 1991
The Home Front: Propaganda, Fiona Reynoldson, Wayland, 1991
Codes, Ciphers and Secret Writing, Martin Gardner, Dover Publications, 1985
Hiroshima: The Shadow of the Bomb, Richard Tames, Heinemann Library, 1999

Fiction

The Silver Sword, Ian Serraillier, Puffin Books, 1993
Carrie's War, Nina Bawden, Puffin Books, 2000
Echoes of War, Robert Westall, Puffin Books, 1995
The Machine Gunners, Robert Westall, Macmillan, 1994

Websites

World War Two encyclopedia site:
    www.spartacus.schoolnet.co.uk/2WW.htm
World War Two website:
    http://school.discovery.com/homeworkhelp/worldbook/atozhistory/w/610460.html
Website of the Imperial War Museum, London, a major repository of World War Two
    documents and artefacts:
    www.iwm.org.uk/

Places of interest

Imperial War Museum, London
HMS *Belfast* (World War Two cruiser), London
RAF Museum and American Air Museum, Duxford
Spitfire and Hurricane Memorial Building, RAF Manston, Kent
Kent Battle of Britain Museum, Hawkinge, Kent
Bovington Tank Museum, Dorset
Fleet Air Arm Museum, Yeovilton
Bletchley Park Trust (World War Two cipher centre), Milton Keynes

Glossary

ammunition bullets, shells, missiles, grenades and anything else fired during fighting

amphibious operating on land and in water

amplify increase the strength of a signal, such as a radio signal, or other noise

anti-bacterial able to kill bacteria

antibiotic medicine that fights infection

armour plating thick metal sheets to protect a tank or ship, for example, against shells and bullets

artillery large guns

ballistic missile guided long-range self-propelled missile

barrage barrier against an enemy action. An artillery barrage is a barrier of heavy shellfire used to cover one's own side in an attack or defend against an enemy attack.

barrel tube of a gun through which ammunition is fired

bayonet metal blade attached to a gun

casualty wounded or killed person

caterpillar track revolving steel band, made up of joined sections, that is used instead of wheels for vehicles that travel on rough ground or in mud

civilian citizen of a country who is not in the armed forces

commando soldier trained to carry out operations behind enemy lines

convoy group of ships travelling together with an armed escort

cryptanalyst specialist in devising and breaking codes

detonate make something explode

dive-bomber aircraft that releases its bombs while diving towards its target

electromechanical using electricity to operate switches and other parts

electronic relating to electrons, the basic particles of electricity, and used to describe devices using electronic power

element one of about 100 simple substances that make up all other substances

empire territory, usually covering more than one country or area, ruled by an emperor or other supreme ruler

epidemic disease spreading rapidly and affecting many people at once

evacuate get people out of a particular area in an emergency situation

firestorm unstoppable blaze sometimes produced when air is sucked into an area set on fire by bombs

flak exploding anti-aircraft shells. From the German for anti-aircraft defence.

front line the foremost section of an army's defended territory and the most exposed to the enemy

fuse device that sets off an explosion

genocide systematic destruction of a national, racial or religious group

glider aeroplane without an engine

grenade small explosive device either thrown by hand or fired from a launcher

guided missile weapon that travels through the air or water directed by remote control

home front situation or contributions of civilians in a nation at war

howitzer type of gun which fires shells on a high trajectory

incendiary bomb bomb designed to set fire to buildings or other targets

infantry soldiers who fight on foot

innovation something new or changed

insecticide chemical that kills insects

jam block or confuse radio signals so they become unreadable

laser device for producing a beam of light capable of travelling vast distances

manoeuvrable easy to move, turn or control in other ways

offensive used for attacking. Also means a large pre-planned attack.

periscope instrument with which a person can observe from a concealed position, such as from a submerged submarine or over the top of a wall

piston engine engine using a piston and piston-rod. The piston is a disc or cylinder that moves up and down inside a tube to create motion.

quinine anti-malarial drug extracted from the bark of a tropical tree

radar system that detects and locates objects by bouncing radio waves off them

radiation sending out of rays, especially used to refer to large amounts of rays harmful to people

radiation sickness damage to body tissue resulting from exposure to nuclear radiation

recoil spring back after being fired

reconnaissance military observation to assess an enemy's strength and movement

reinforcements extra support, such as new men or weapons brought into a battle

rifle long-barrelled firearm which has a rifled (spirally grooved) barrel. This spins the bullet being fired, to give it both longer range and greater accuracy.

rocket projectile that carries its own oxygen supply to burn fuel

round bullet and cartridge. The cartridge contains an explosive charge to propel the bullet from the gun, and is ejected once the bullet has been fired.

shells metal cases of various shapes containing explosives or other harmful materials

sonar (short for <u>so</u>und <u>na</u>vigation and <u>r</u>anging) system that detects and locates objects underwater through the use of soundwaves

stalemate situation where both sides in a conflict are unable to defeat each other

strategy overall plan for dealing with a conflict or a battle

strongpoint defensive position on battlefront that has extra fortifications or weapons

supersonic faster than the speed of sound

technology knowledge and ability that improves ways of doing practical things

telegraph device for sending messages along wires

trajectory path taken by an object as it flies through the air

transfusion injection of blood into a wounded person to replace blood lost in an injury

turret small tower on a tank or ship that holds and protects guns and gunners.

vacuum tube tube from which air has been removed that was used as an amplifier in early electronic devices

velocity speed of an object's movement

warhead the part of a missile containing an explosive charge

Index

aeroplanes 4, 5, 10, 13, 16, 17, 19, 20, 21, 26, 31, 34, 35, 36, 39, 42, 43
  bombers 5, 12, 13, 14–15, 19, 20, 23, 26, 27, 36
  fighters 12–13, 20, 23, 26, 27
  gliders 16, 17
  jets 5, 13, 43
airborne troops 16–17
aircraft carriers 5, 19, 20–21, 25
Allies 4, 10, 11, 13, 15, 17, 19, 22, 23, 24, 25, 26, 27, 31, 34, 35, 36, 37, 39, 40, 41
amphibious vehicles 11, 22, 23
anti-aircraft weapons 9, 14, 18, 20, 36
antibiotics 5, 41, 43
anti-radar devices 27
anti-submarine weapons 19, 25
anti-tank weapons 7, 9, 11
artificial harbours 23
artillery 8–9, 10, 27, 28
artillery barrages 9
Axis Powers 4, 5

ballistic missiles 5, 37, 42
Battle of the Atlantic 24, 25
Battle of Britain 12–13, 14, 26, 36
battleships 18, 19, 20, 25
bayonets 6
bazookas 7
blitzkrieg 4, 10, 28
blood plasma 40
Bohr, Neils 38
bombs 14, 15, 41
  atomic 5, 38–39, 42
  bouncing 15
Braun, Wernher von 37
Britain 4, 12, 14, 17, 18, 19, 23, 24, 25, 26, 27, 36

Canada 4, 38
carbines 6
casualties 15, 17, 22, 25, 33, 36, 39, 40, 41, 42
Churchill, Winston 5, 33
code-breaking 25, 30–31
communications 17, 25, 27, 28–29, 43
computers 5, 30, 31, 42, 43
Coral Sea 21

depth-charges 24, 25
Drew, Charles 40

Einstein, Albert 38, 39
Enigma 30, 31

Fleming, Alexander 41
France 4, 5, 10, 14, 17, 23, 31, 37

Germany 4, 5, 7, 10, 13, 15, 24, 25, 27, 28, 32, 34, 35, 36, 37, 38, 39, 42, 43
Goebbels, Josef 32, 33, 34
grenades 7
Guderian, General Hans 28
guided missiles 36, 37

Harris, Air-Marshall 'Bomber' 14
Haw-Haw, Lord 33
Hiroshima 39
Hitler, Adolf 4, 10, 12, 13, 16, 17, 19, 31, 33, 34, 36, 37, 39
home front 5, 34–35
howitzers 8

illness and infection 39, 40, 41, 43
insecticides 5, 41, 43
Italy 4, 11, 22, 41

Japan 4, 11, 13, 18, 20, 21, 22, 25, 31, 33, 35, 39, 42
Jeeps 7

kamikaze missions 15

landing craft 22, 23
land-mines 7
Liberty ships 34
Luftwaffe 12, 13

machine guns 6
Manhattan Project 38
medicine 40–41
Midway Island 21, 31, 33
mines, underwater 19
Montgomery, Bernard 28
mortars 8, 29
Mussolini, Benito 17

Nagasaki 39
Nazis 4, 24, 32, 33, 34, 35, 39

Normandy invasion 11, 17, 22, 23, 31, 40, 41
nuclear weapons 38, 39, 42, 43

Oppenheimer, J Robert 38

Pacific Ocean 4, 19, 20, 21, 22, 25, 31, 35, 39, 40
parachutes 16, 17
Patton, General George 28
Pearl Harbor 18, 19, 20, 25
pistols 6
propaganda 32–33

radar 5, 25, 26–27, 36, 42, 43
radio 5, 25, 27, 28, 29, 30, 32, 33
rifles 6
rockets 9, 36–37, 42
Roosevelt, Franklin D 33, 38, 39
Royal Air Force 12, 13, 14, 19, 26, 27

secret codes 21, 25, 30–31
shells 8, 10, 18, 37
south-east Asia 11, 33, 40
Soviet Union 4, 7, 10, 35, 37, 42
Stalin, Josef 4, 35
Streicher, Julius 33
sub-machine guns 6–7
submarines 5, 19, 24–25, 42
synthetic fuel 35
synthetic rubber 35, 43

tanks 4, 5, 7, 8, 9, 10–11, 28, 29, 43
Tokyo Rose 33
torpedoes 19, 20
Truman, Harry 39

U-boats 24, 25, 31, 42
United States of America 4, 7, 18, 19, 21, 22, 25, 29, 31, 34, 35, 37, 38, 39, 40, 42, 43

Wallis, Barnes 15
war industry 5, 14, 15, 34, 35, 37
warships 5, 18–19, 20, 23, 25, 31
World War One 4, 6, 8, 12, 18, 29, 40

Yamamoto, Isoroku 20, 21, 31

Titles in the *20th Century Perspectives* series include:

Hardback   0 431 11994 5

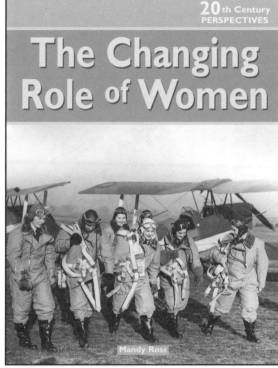

Hardback   0 431 11997 X

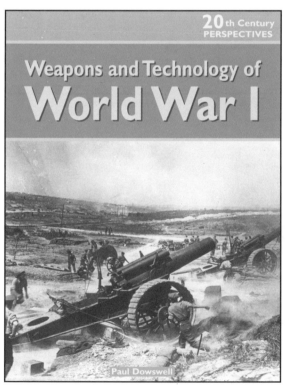

Hardback   0 431 11995 3

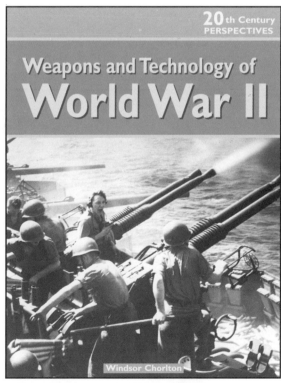

Hardback   0 431 11996 1

Find out about the other titles in this series on our website www.heinemann.co.uk/library